A friend is one of life's most beautiful gifts.

🌿 *Luann Auciello*

Friendship

A Blue Mountain Arts® Collection
for a Friend Who Means
the World to Me

Edited by Diane Mastromarino

Blue Mountain Press™

Boulder, Colorado

We wish to thank Susan Polis Schutz for permission to reprint the following poems
that appear in this publication: "There are many people..." and "Sometimes we are
lucky enough...." Copyright © 1983, 1988 by Stephen Schutz and Susan Polis
Schutz. All rights reserved.

Library of Congress Control Number: 2003099549
ISBN: 0-88396-838-X

Certain trademarks are used under license.
BLUE MOUNTAIN PRESS is registered in U.S. Patent and Trademark Office.

Manufactured in Thailand.
First Printing: 2004

 This book is printed on recycled paper.

Blue Mountain Arts, Inc.

P.O. Box 4549, Boulder, Colorado 80306

Contents

(Authors listed in order of first appearance)

To Find a Friend Is a Wonderful Joy...

A friend can guide you, inspire you, comfort you, or light up your life with laughter. A friend is a gift that brings happiness, and a treasure that money can't buy.

➤ *Collin McCarty*

Sometimes in life,
you find a special friend:
someone who changes your life
by being a part of it.
Someone who makes you laugh
until you can't stop.
Someone who makes you believe
that there really is good in the world.
Someone who convinces you
that there is an unlocked door
just waiting for you to open it.
This is forever friendship.

When you're down,
and the world seems dark and empty,
your forever friend lifts you up in spirit
and makes that dark and empty world
suddenly seem bright and full.

Your forever friend gets you through
the hard times, the sad times,
and the confused times.
If you turn and walk away,
your forever friend follows.
If you lose your way,
your forever friend guides you
and cheers you on.
Your forever friend holds your hand
and tells you that
everything is going to be okay.
And if you find such a friend,
you feel happy and complete,
because you need not worry.
You have a forever friend for life,
and forever has no end.

🌱 Laurieann Kelly

Of all the means to insure happiness throughout the whole of life, by far the most important is... friends.

— *Epicurus*

*F*riendship begins with meeting someone along the path of life. Someone you get to know, and gradually get to know even better. You discover what a joy it is to spend your moments with this person.

As the good feelings of friendship grow, the happiness increases and the memories you make start to turn into some of your favorite treasures. Friendship is two paths converging on the way to the same beautiful view. It is walking the way together.

Friendship is opening up to one another. Sharing thoughts and feelings in a way that never felt very comfortable before. It is a complete trust, sweetened with a lot more understanding and communication than many people will ever know.

Friendship is two hearts that share and which are able to say things no outsiders ever could. It is an inner door that only a friend has the key to. Friendship is a gift, continually giving happiness. It is strong and supportive, and few things in all the world will ever compare with the joy that comes from its wonderful bond.

❧ Mia Evans

We cannot tell the precise moment when friendship is formed. As in filling a vessel drop by drop, there is at last a drop which makes it run over; so in a series of kindnesses there is at last one which makes the heart run over.

James Boswell

*T*he first time I met you, I knew we would be friends. We connected immediately with mutual interests and easy, natural conversations. When we're together, I feel relaxed and comfortable. I am more myself with you than I am with anyone else I know.

I love how we laugh and have fun together. We never run out of things to talk about. I confide in you with complete faith and trust. Your friendship has brought a new sense of peace into my life. It has allowed me to examine my own life and graciously taught me how to be gentler with the person I am.

Your friendship has brought me a newfound sense of confidence and self-worth. It has given me a special love that remains loyal and true. As a friend, you've given me a piece of your heart. I am fortunate to be blessed with the wonderful experiences we've had. I am deeply honored to have you as my friend.

➤ Debbie Burton-Peddle

True friendship is that unexplained heart connection between two people who enrich each other's life. They may not know exactly why they became friends, but they do know that their presence in each other's life is a gift.

— *Donna Fargo*

*T*here's something so special
about our friendship —
the way we know
what the other is thinking
the way we can talk for hours
without ever feeling
the time pass us by
It is a comfort to know
that I can turn to you for anything
and never worry
about what you will say
or how you will make me feel
You have a way of always finding
the right words
and if there are no words
the silence we share has this way
of making everything okay
I'm so glad that I have you
to turn to when life doesn't go
exactly as planned
and more so
I am glad that I have you
to celebrate the wonderful times with
Your friendship is something
I am thankful for each and every day

— Elle Mastro

True Friends Come Along Once in a Lifetime

A friend is a living treasure, and
if you have one, you have one of
the most valuable gifts in life.

— *Collin McCarty*

Sometimes we are lucky enough
to meet a person
who stands out
among all the other people
as being extremely special
who knows what we
are thinking about
who is happy for us at all times
who is always there to talk to us
who cares about us selflessly
who is always truthful with us
Sometimes we are lucky enough
to meet someone who is
extremely wonderful
For me
that person
is you
my dear friend

— Susan Polis Schutz

*F*riends like you are angels
sent down to earth
to make good days...

and help us find our way.

✖ *Ashley Rice*

You Are like an Angel to Me

In this life, on this earth, and in the days that I spend trying to do the best I can, I know that I wouldn't be half the person I am if it weren't for a little divine inspiration that comes from having a friend like you.

You are my friend, my see-me-through and inspire-my-smile companion. When you listen, you hear what I'm really trying to say. And when you communicate, your words come straight from the heart.

You are so amazing. Compared to you, I feel like I'll always be in training for my own set of wings. You are my very own down-to-earth angel. I cherish you very much, and I want to thank you, my dear friend, for the way you bring so much joy to my life.

— Marin McKay

There are many people
that we meet in our lives
but only a very few
will make a lasting impression
on our minds and hearts
It is these people that we will
think of often
and who will always remain
important to us
as true friends

➤ *Susan Polis Schutz*

I am grateful
for many things and many people,
but especially for you.
You have touched my life
and my world in a way that
few others have ever done,
and I know I will never be the same.
You have brightened my life
with the gifts of your laughter and joy
and the comfort of knowing someone cares.
You have stood strong for me
when the rest of the world
seemed not to care.
You have been my true friend
when I had very little friendship
to give back.
You have taken the time to listen
when I needed to talk,
and to hug me when I cried.
You have given me yourself,
the very best gift of all.

❧ Donna Surgenor Reames

You're the Friend Who Is Always in My Heart

You're the friend who has always been there for me through the years, with arms full of caring and a heart full of love.

You're the friend who has loved me unconditionally — accepting me as I am, never wanting to change me into somebody I'm not.

You're the friend who has given me advice when I've needed it, the one who has turned my tears into laughter more times than I can count.

You're the friend who has shown me how wonderful people can be, how filled with kindness and compassion and love some hearts are.

You're the friend who has proven to me that love can last forever and that friendship is one of life's most certain guarantees.

You're the friend who means everything to me, the one who will always be in my heart.

— Rachyl Taylor

Friendship Is a Shoulder to Lean On and a Place to Be Yourself

We have been friends together
in sunshine and in shade.

— *Caroline Elizabeth Sarah Norton*

$\mathcal{F}$riends are the special people who walk with you through life, sharing in whatever the days may bring, making the dark times seem brighter and the happy times even more memorable.

Friends are always there with unconditional love and understanding, encouraging even the wildest of your dreams, picking you up if you fall, and giving you the strength and the courage to try again. They are the rays of light in your warmest memories, the laughter and the smiles that will live in your heart forever.

— Rachyl Taylor

A friend is someone who offers
understanding when life is difficult,
someone whose smile is enough
to brighten any day,
someone who accepts you
and is glad that you are you.

➤ *Donna Levine Small*

*A*lthough the fun we have is
a wonderful part of our friendship,
it is only one of the many things
I have come to value about you.
I've had the opportunity to experience
your spirit, loyalty,
and sense of understanding.
I admire the passion with which
you live your days
and the kindness you display
toward others.
I've learned I can depend
on your strength,
and I can trust in your advice
and direction.
I've discovered these unique qualities
over time —
and knowing all this about you
makes me especially thankful
you came into my life.

           ✴ Nicole Jung

*F*riends are part of who we are
They make a difference in our lives
They offer us the comfort of knowing
someone understands
and the satisfaction of knowing
we have something to believe in

— *Shannon M. Lester*

*I*n everyday life, it's so important to have someone to relax with, to be yourself with, to talk freely with, and not feel you have to entertain constantly. Our friendship is like that.

We don't try to change each other or improve each other; we accept each other. I appreciate our friendship so much. I've come to value your thoughtfulness and constancy, and I'm thankful for your sensitivity and loyalty.

Because we're so supportive of each other, we have grown closer in time. When we've needed reassurance, we always let each other know that we're there for the long term, and that really means a lot to me.

I feel so lucky to have you for a friend.

— Donna Fargo

Your friend is the one who knows all about you, and still likes you.

— Elbert Hubbard

With You I Can Just Be Me

With you, I don't have to be fancy or talk in a special way. I don't have to mind my manners or wear my best clothes and shoes. I don't have to pretend I'm happy when I'm feeling sad. I don't have to count calories or act like I'm someone I'm not.

With you I can cry, I can laugh out loud. I can speak my mind or say nothing at all, depending on my mood. I don't have to try hard to impress you or think of important things to say. With you, everything is important.

With you, I can just be me... and I really appreciate you for that.

— Elle Mastro

Friendship grows Stronger Through the Years...

As gold more splendid
from the fire appears;
Thus friendship brightens
by length of years.

Thomas Carlyle

*T*here is something so special
about a friend who has been there
through so many years.
You've watched me change and grow,
experiencing all the stages of life
right along with me.
No one else will ever know me
the way you do.
No one else will ever share
all those memories of laughter and tears,
growing and changing,
living and loving.
As the years have passed by,
I've met many new people
and made many new friends.
But there will always be
a space in my heart
that can never be filled
by anyone but you.

— Rachyl Taylor

Ours Is a
Lifelong Friendship

In this chaotic world where it seems we constantly race to catch today, an enduring friendship such as ours didn't just happen — we built it moment by moment, year after year, with understanding and sacrifice, care and trust, tears and love.

I wish I could discover new words to tell you how deeply thankful I am for your never-ending friendship. But some feelings are not meant for words; some feelings are more eloquently expressed silently, heart to heart, soul to soul.

Although our life journeys sometimes take us far apart and down different paths, when your life changes, so does mine. I believe our willingness to encourage and embrace the changing aspects of each other's life continually strengthens and renews our special bond.

You are the truest friend I have ever known. Whatever courses our lives take, always remember that there will never be a day that I do not think of you, pray for you, and send you my love.

— E. M. Uso

*F*riends are the joys
that make us more like family.
They are candles lit by one another...
the glow of time and memory
to warm our hearts.

Linda E. Knight

I have always seen my life
as a journey on a road to tomorrow.
There have been hills and valleys
and turns here and there
that have filled my life with
all kinds of challenges and changes.
But I made it through those times,
because there were always
special friends I met along the way.
My special friends
are the ones who
have walked beside me,
comforting my spirit or
holding my hand
when I needed it most.
They were friends who
loved my smiles
and were not afraid of my tears.
They were true friends
who really cared about me.
Those friends are forever;
they are cherished and loved
more than they'll ever know.

— Deanna Beisser

I Can't Imagine
My Life Without You

*A*s my friend, you are the one person
who shares my deepest thoughts
And loves me in spite of them.
You counsel me when my
    heart is broken,
And you stand by me when I'm mistreated.
You rally behind me in my good decisions
And are there to help me through
    the consequences of the bad ones.
Whom else can I call at any hour
    of the day or night?
Who else accepts and understands all of me?
Not many people are as blessed as I am
With someone like you in their life.

I don't know why the heavens decided
    to give me
The wonderful gift of you as my friend,
But I'm grateful.
No matter what comes along, good or bad,
It brings me great comfort and security
To know that I can always count on you.
I hope you know in your heart that
I am that same sort of friend to you.
Our secrets are safe
    and our hearts are protected
Because of the love between us...
Two special friends.

— Pamela Malone-Melton

Friendship Is Forever...

Of all the gifts life may bestow,
none is so constant, steady, and sure
as the tender heart of a friend.

— *Robert Sexton*

We've been friends for a long time.
Our hearts are interlocked,
and what we are together
makes us stronger
and helps us persevere.
Together we've tried our wings;
we've soared high, crashed,
celebrated, and cried.
We've dried each other's tears
and picked up the pieces
    of broken dreams.
Together, we've made things
better than they were before.
It's not even so much the help
    we've given each other;
it's the absolute confidence
that we will always be there —
wanting, willing, and ready
    to help... always and forever.

❧ Vickie M. Worsham

*F*riends forever remain a part of your life — whether you see them every day or only when they drift in and out through the years.

➤ *Jane Andrews*

No matter where we go,
we always remember
the wonderful people who touched our lives
and who loved us and helped us
learn more about ourselves.
We always remember
the people who stayed by us
when we had to face difficult times
and with whom we felt safe enough
to reveal our true selves.
Friends are the unforgettable people
we dream and plan
great futures with,
who accept us as we are
and encourage us to become
all that we want to be.

My friend,
no matter where we go in life
or how far apart we are,
you will always be close to me,
and I will always be your friend.

— Donna Levine Small

Good friends are the kind of friends who stand by each other no matter what. When they say they mean forever, they really do.

— Donna Fargo

*T*here will always be a special place in my heart... for you. It is a place that knows how very much there is to appreciate about you. About your giving and your sharing. About your beautiful spirit and your kind and caring soul. About the generous way you manage to brighten so many days.

It is a place that is filled with warm and thankful feelings. Feelings that understand how seldom someone like you comes along.

It is a place that inspires a more positive outlook on everything every time I think of you. Within my heart is a place that recognizes your uniqueness and celebrates the blessing of the friendship we share.

— Douglas Pagels

Friends like Us
Are Forever

Friends like us don't need to see each other every day... No matter how long it's been since we were last together, we just pick up right where we left off.

Friends like us don't need to ask for help... We just know that we'll always be there for each other, anytime, anywhere.

Friends like us don't need to apologize for our bad days or our bad moods... We just understand that life isn't always the brightest, and we take turns cheering each other up.

Friends like us don't need to worry about what to say, how to act, or what to wear... We feel comfortable enough to be ourselves and know that we're loved just the way we are.

Friends like us don't need to hide how we're feeling... We can act as crazy and silly as we want without worrying what the other person will think.

Friends like us don't need to tell each other how much we care... We can just feel the strength of our friendship in our hearts.

Friends like us... are forever.

— Rachyl Taylor

ACKNOWLEDGMENTS

We gratefully acknowledge the permission granted by the following authors and authors' representatives to reprint poems or excerpts from their publications.

Debbie Burton-Peddle for "The first time I met you...." Copyright © 2004 by Debbie Burton-Peddle. All rights reserved.

PrimaDonna Entertainment Corp. for "Good friends are the kind...," "True friendship is that unexplained...," and "In everyday life..." by Donna Fargo. Copyright © 2002, 2003, 2004 by PrimaDonna Entertainment Corp. All rights reserved.

Nicole Jung for "Although the fun we have is...." Copyright © 2004 by Nicole Jung. All rights reserved.

Robert Sexton for "Of all the gifts life may bestow..." from ALL THE WAY HOME. Copyright © 1992 by Robert Sexton. All rights reserved.

Vickie M. Worsham for "We've been friends for a long time." Copyright © 2004 by Vickie M. Worsham. All rights reserved.

A careful effort has been made to trace the ownership of selections used in this anthology in order to obtain permission to reprint copyrighted material and give proper credit to the copyright owners. If any error or omission has occurred, it is completely inadvertent, and we would like to make corrections in future editions provided that written notification is made to the publisher:

BLUE MOUNTAIN ARTS, INC., P.O. Box 4549, Boulder, Colorado 80306.